Elizabeth
Lord Bless you in
your work !
2.26.99

Blessed is the Meadow

Stories of the Spiritual Lives
of People with Developmental Disability

by

Barbara Esch Shisler

Pen and Ink Illustrations
by Julie Longacre

Cover Painting
by Jake Deery

Indian Creek Foundation
573 Yoder Road
P.O. Box 225
Harleysville, Pa. 19438-0228

Unless otherwise noted, the Bible text is from the New Revised Standard Version Bible, ©1989, by the Division of Christian Education of the National Council of the Churches of Christ in the USA, and is used by permission.

Cover painting by Jake Deery, Souderton Mennonite Homes, for "Brush With Harmony," 1997, with Julie Longacre

Book design and pen and ink illustrations by Julie Longacre

Photo credits: Merle Landes, page 16
                    Tom Moyer, page 10
                    Marilyn Nolt, page 46

Quote credits:
Julian of Norwich, page 20, from "Revelations of Divine Love"
Rachel Miller Jacobs, page 17, from *Gospel Herald*
Previously published material, pages 15 and 68, *Gospel Herald*

Copyright ©1998 Indian Creek Foundation
                    573 Yoder Road, P.O. Box 225
                    Harleysville, Pennsylvania 19438-0225
                    215-256-1500

Library of Congress Catalog Card Number: 98-73775
ISBN 0-9667045-0-9

Printed by Smale's Printery, Pottstown, Pa. 19464

CONTENTS

Acknowledgements iv
Foreword vi
Introduction ix

1. Blessed Are the Poor in Spirit 11
   -Violet, Elizabeth, Anita

2. Blessed Are Those Who Mourn 17
   -Karen, Craig, Sherry, Scott

3. Blessed Are the Meek 23
   -Chris, Paula, Orlando, Mary Ann

4. Blessed Are Those Who Hunger and 29
   and Thirst for Righteousness
   -Joyce, Barbara, Linda, Sterling, Bob

5. Blessed Are the Merciful 35
   -Ron, Ed, Mildred

6. Blessed Are the Pure in Heart 39
   -Dick, Della, Mark, Four Women

7. Blessed Are the Peacemakers 47
   -Richard, Mary Kathryn, Leonard,
   Laverne, Paul, William

8. Blessed Are Those Who Are Persecuted 53
   -Trish, Brad, Clifford

9. You Are the Salt of the Earth 59
   -Allen, B.J.

10. You Are the Light of the World 65
    -Faith and Light

Afterword 70

ACKNOWLEDGEMENTS

I wish to thank:

♦ Indian Creek Foundation for support and encouragement in bringing this book into being. Thanks especially to Mindy Moyer for her generous encouragement and help. Thanks to Jennifer Bartos for her hours of computer work on the manuscript. Thanks to Greg Bowman for his careful editing and affirming words.

♦ Those who shared their lives and their stories with me and gave permission to publish their stories, prayers and photographs in this book. Thanks to the family members who gave permissions.

♦ B.J. Diehl for the use of her poems and for checking in with me often about how the book was progressing.

♦ Julie Longacre for book design and illustrations and for her helpful perspectives in working with the printer. Julie has a bachelor of fine arts degree from Bethany College, Lindsborg, Kansas.

♦ Dawn Ruth Nelson, my colleague at Indian Creek, who suggested that I get started on this project that had long been in my heart.

Thanks be to God.

DEDICATION

I dedicate this book to
all my brothers and sisters
whom I have come to know and love
through Indian Creek Foundation
and Faith and Light.
They have shown me the way to live
in the meadow of God's kingdom.

FOREWORD

On November 17, 1958, Allen Gehman was born into the family of Anna and Harley and their three daughters. Anna's unease with the odd limpness of the new baby received only a vague response from the doctor. But as she lifted him to her shoulder one morning she caught a glimpse of his profile and knew that her son had Downs Syndrome. Thus began a journey that was to touch the lives of a wide eastern Pennsylvania community.

Not much was available in those years for children with mental retardation. But Anna was vigorous, a home-maker who did not let grass grow peacefully under her feet. Allen's birth gave her a new vision—to work at organizing and supporting services for people with disabilities. Her questions for Allen— where was he going to live, where was he going to work— spurred her on to find answers for others in similar situations.

Allen's first school was the Wrens Nursery, a county-operated preschool for children with developmental disabilities who could not attend public school until the age of eight. He was taken struggling and sobbing at age two and a half, for early training is imperative for children with mental retardation. Just when Anna was ready to give up and keep Allen at home, he adjusted and stayed happily at school.

The church was vital to Gehman family life. Anna's energies naturally focused on Sunday School. She organized Hilltop Sunday School for children with developmental disabilities in 1962 in a building on a farm formerly used by Franconia Mennonite Conference in Harleysville, Pa., for a mission to alcoholics. The Sunday School grew to include 25 children from the surrounding community. Hilltop Sunday School continues nearby at Salford Mennonite Church where adults now meet weekly for religious teaching and fellowship.

New programs developed slowly with Anna's energies ever simmering. "Sometimes I felt like a broken record," she said. "Some people thought I had a one-track mind."

Foster care for disabled persons began. A workshop was started in 1968 for training disabled people in such basic skills as packaging products for local companies and summer gardening. The Brotherhood Commission of Franconia Mennonite Conference invited Paul Glanzer from Virginia to take charge of the shop in a barn on the Indian Creek farm. The former Hilltop Sunday School building became the first group home with eight residents. Joe Landis was hired as the first executive director for an organization that was to oversee the workshop and residential programs.

In 1975, Indian Creek Homes was launched with Harley Gehman on the board. Later, Anna also served on the board, and both were tireless volunteers. In 1990, Indian Creek Foundation became the parent company of Indian Creek Homes and Indian Creek Industries. The Industries program went beyond the workshop model to provide vocational training for community jobs. Family Services began in order to help keep disabled persons with their families when it seemed best. Over time came Congregational Services, Friendship Volunteers,

Summer Camp, a Graduate Program, and a Community Farm Project. Anna's vision took off as Joe Landis and others dreamed big and worked hard to make it a reality.

Today Indian Creek Foundation serves more than 90 persons in its residential program, 151 in industries, 188 in Family Services. Congregational Services is now a full-time pastoral service that connects those interested to nearly 30 area congregations. Pastoral care for core members and staff, three weekly chapel services, educational outreach, and support resources for congregations help meet the spiritual needs of interested persons.

The stories in this book grow out of my 10 years as a pastor at Indian Creek. The spiritual lives of the core members who shared their experiences of God with me are treasured gifts I want to pass on to others. Indian Creek began with a family, and continues to be family for core members, but also for staff and volunteers who find hospitality and welcome there.

—*B.E.S.*

Indian Creek will always be my home,
This home will always live by love.
Hard time we share each other.
Some time we walk in valley of the pasture.
I always be thankful.

—*B.J. Diehl*

INTRODUCTION

The writer of the Gospel of Matthew included in the narrative a "Sermon on the Mount." This discourse is at the heart of the teachings of Jesus. The Sermon begins with a set of Beatitudes, proclamations which declare God's favor or blessedness for those who make their home in the community of God.

The Jerusalem Bible translates blessed as "happy." I like happy. I grew up believing it was not important to be happy as long as I was faithful. But a sad faithfulness makes faith a burden. Happiness, with its wellspring of joy, makes faith a true delight that brings peace and fulfillment.

The friends with developmental disabilities who have shared their faith with me are Beatitude people. God's favor belongs to them through their openness, trust, and simplicity. They have much to teach about the wisdom of God versus the wisdom of the world. Though trouble, sorrow, and anger are painfully a part of their lives, blessedness and happiness is promised them.

The meadow is an image of simplicity, beauty, and peace. There, goodness makes a home in the creatureliness that brings heaven and earth in harmony, that rejoices in the reality and the promise of God's purpose for all creation.

—Barbara Esch Shisler
August 1998

1

Blessed are the poor in spirit,
for theirs is the kingdom of heaven.

Blessed are those who know their own need
and are not afraid to ask for help.
The Psalmist must have been a soul poor in spirit.
Crying out for help reverberates through those poems.
Help me… save me… protect me… rescue me.

Why am I so reluctant to admit I'm weak and needy?
Why do I buy into a culture that says,
"Hide your littleness, for independence is most admired?"
"You become strong by pretending to be strong."
"Don't ask for help."
"Don't admit you are crying inside."
"Just put on your 'I'm fine' face, and carry on."

("You don't really need the kingdom of heaven.")

Happy is the meadow
whose simple spirit
asks only to hug the ground
of the kingdom of heaven.

VIOLET. Her name names the bright little flower that blooms close to the ground, spreading persistent roots, stepped on and mowed off, but not deterred.

Now 80, Violet came to us from years in the state hospital without family or friends. But she needs family; she seeks her people.

"There's my Sister Honey!" she cries, beckoning me for a vigorous hug and resounding kiss.

"There's my Uncle."

"There's my People."

Receiving cards is a sign of peoplehood. "Send me a birthday card," she says at Christmas. "Send me a Christmas card," she says at Easter. "Did you send my Valentine yet?" she asks at Halloween. It doesn't matter what or when. Receiving the card assures her that she belongs to someone, she's loved.

On a bitter December day she insists on sitting by the outside door at workshop waiting for her People to come by and take her home for Christmas. She waits and waits, reassuring herself in a low and hopeful voice that they will come. But finally she is too cold and agrees to go back and join the group.

One day at chapel she picked up the icon of Jesus from the altar. "I love the dear Lord," she said, kissing it. "Isn't he pretty?"

Then she leads out in her favorite of all songs:

> *Jesus loves me this I know,*
> *for the Bible tells me so,*
> *little ones to him belong,*
> *they are weak but he is strong.*

ELIZABETH. Liz. She embodies a beautiful fragility. Her blue eyes gaze from a young face framed with curly brown hair. The fragility can turn to outraged vengeance quickly, unexpectedly.

We are going together to Mass. Her church is some miles from her group home so we have time to talk on the way. Liz fills me in on all that's wrong in her world. She shouts. Curses. Cries. I wonder if going to church today is a good idea.

We enter the sanctuary of St. Philips. The quietness, dignity, reverence sink in. "I am a good Catholic girl," she told me once. The good Catholic girl kneels when it's appropriate, stands to sing, repeats the prayers, goes forward without me to receive Communion.

As we leave the parking lot the blue eyes in the lovely face turn to me. A small smile plays around her mouth. "Now the Lord is in my heart," she whispers.

ANITA had been away from church attendance since childhood. Now as a young adult her disabilities continued to prevent her attending.

But "Little Group" gave her another chance. Held in a church sanctuary for a short sensory half hour of lively singing with rhythm instruments, visual and auditory helps, things to touch and smell and taste, it allowed Anita to participate.

The first time she came, she bounded down the aisle unmindful of her disabled feet to the front bench, a big smile on her face.

She cried during the singing, signed "drink" as though remembering Communion.

She reached out gently to touch the cross and the icon of Jesus. Though unable to speak, her vocal sounds were ones of recognition and joy.

Anita, multiply disabled, poor in body and mind, rich in the spirit that opens itself like a little child to God, through your too early death, you have entered fully into the Kingdom that belongs to you.

⌘⌘⌘

Dear Jesus,
Be with Jan if she takes me out for my birthday in March,
Be with Jan if she's able to take me out next time she comes, in Jesus' name amen;
Pray Joe Landis will take me to his church on Sunday,
I hope I have a good birthday in March,
Be with my mom and dad in Jesus' name amen;
Maybe they'll be able to drive up here Sunday to take me out, in Jesus' name, Amen.

—Annie

Gathering Around the Table of God

Communion has been announced for this Faith and Light meeting.* A joyful ripple moves around the circle. No one in this "church" is blasé about communion.

The majority of worshippers are disabled in some way. People with wheelchairs and walkers find their places. People who talk oddly or talk at the wrong time or don't talk at all bring their language to the worship. We are serving the body broken for us all. What more appropriate place for broken bodies to gather than around the disabled Christ?

Bob picks up a stray guitar and does an impromptu song while the bread is being served. So we listen to Bob. John spills his wine on the communion cloth. Now we will remember John. Judy has a seizure and leans across her neighbor's lap until it passes. Now we care for Judy. Whatever is happening here is happening in the presence and protection of love. It is all blessed.

We are one body formed through the broken body, made up of many parts. How tenderly we respond to the vulnerable part; how respectful we are of what is at risk of being cast aside. When my disabled sister's gift of friendship is ignored, I am as wounded as she. If my brother makes unexpected sounds, I receive that sound as his personal expression, for this is a place for recognition, not rejection.

Shirley picks up a bit of bread that fell to the floor. She looks at it knowingly, then pops it into her mouth. The word made flesh dwells among us. And we behold and marvel at grace and truth.

*For a description of Faith and Light, see p. 65.

2

Blessed are those who mourn,
for they will be comforted.

"Mourning is an embracing of our losses...to mourn is to see loss as an invitation to dive in and plumb its depths, to enter into it fully." (Rachel Miller Jacobs in *Gospel Herald,* 11/11/97)

Death is an acceptable experience to grieve, but there are many losses to grieve besides death. Life is a series of losses, because each new vista leaves an old one behind. People with developmental disabilities have much to grieve. Their lives change without their choosing. To leave their parents' home as father and mother age or become ill, and move into a group home may be a devastating loss. Even as they become adjusted and contented in their new setting, support persons leave, staff whom they have come to depend on change jobs. Loss is a regular part of life.

Mourning, the active expression and work of grief, is necessary for healing. Sometimes we would wish to protect or avoid those who cannot express their grief in ways we are comfortable with. We can instead learn from those who "dive in and plumb its depths," whose mourning will someday be turned into joy.

Happy are the sorrowing
avoided like thistle
whose tears shall blossom
sweet and purple.

KAREN is sometimes called the "little mother." Slight and intense, her brown eyes piercing behind her smudged glasses, Karen wants to know where everyone of her group home family is, and is going, and when they are returning. Karen keeps track of people who sometimes prefer not to be tracked.

Especially she kept track of Albert.

When Albert died suddenly at the group home, I was called to come at once. I could hear the screaming before I entered the house. I knew it was Karen.

Albert was like her Grandpa. From his white beard to his gentle words, he could have fit a child's image of God. Karen and Albert kept faith with one another. And Karen had gone to Albert's room to call him for dinner and had found him on the floor.

"He wouldn't get up! Why wouldn't he get up?" Karen demanded when I walked into the living room. She was sitting on the floor, held by a resident assistant. "I tried to make him get up… but he wouldn't get up."

For the next two hours, Karen raged. Sometimes she screamed, sometimes she cried, sometimes she pushed everyone away, sometimes she let herself be held and rocked. She regularly shouted threats of the worst things she could imagine for those who had taken Albert from her.

"I'm going to throw that ambulance into the toilet." "I'm going to break that policeman's glasses." These were two of her favorite things to do when life got out of hand.

The official word came from the hospital. I had to say it to those gathered, waiting and hoping. I had to say it to Karen's glaring gaze. She said back to me, "Barbara, will you shut up and go home? Just shut up and go home!"

Blessed are those like Karen who mourn their losses without reservation. Who don't need to be polite in the face of personal tragedy. Who dive fully into the grief and swim toward the comfort of shores.

Blessed are you, Karen, little mother, for you show the way to real mourning.

CRAIG. I hear his voice through the walls that separate the workshop area from my office. It comes periodically like a voice crying in the wilderness, or more wrenching, the voice from the cross.

"I want my Father! I want my Father!"

Father, why have you forsaken me? Why have you abandoned me to suffer alone? I still want to be the little boy in your arms, being tucked into bed by my beloved father. I want the protection of your love more than anything else in the world.

Blessed are you, Craig of the wounded heart. Your cries gather up the collective grief of the world and lift it to heaven.

⌘⌘⌘

SHERRY was blind and deaf and mentally retarded. Her anguish was often expressed in sustained and wracking wails that called to mind the word "keening," a lament for the dead. Sherry's world was indeed death-like, but there were moments and signs of grace.

Sherry was sitting on a sofa with a staff person whose one arm was around her stroking her hair. The staff person's other hand played with Sherry's fingers. The young woman's expression was that of a Madonna. Peace, joy, and love bloomed in her face.

God-signs that even in the most grievous of circumstances, "All shall be well, and all shall be well, and all manner of thing shall be well."

SCOTT says to me, "My Dad died."

Three words tell a story of ongoing grief and loss. Scott's father was a giant of a man, a man whose bigness offered his son a safe and strong harbor for a life frustrated by disability. But suddenly he was gone.

"My Dad died" continues years later. In any setting, at any moment, the wound announces itself. Grief is mourned in simply and clearly stating the profound loss.

Would that comfort, too, might come as profoundly. And yet it will, someday, as Scott's task of mourning goes on.

⌘⌘⌘

Thank you, God, for giving me life,
Thank you, God, for putting me on this earth,
Thank you, God, for giving me Jane to work with me,
Thank you, God, for giving me staff that cares,
Thank you, God, for keeping me living.

God, I hope you are taking care of Daddy.
When I go up there,
then I be with Daddy too. Amen

—Barbara

3

Blessed are the meek,
for they will inherit the earth.

Here's to the gentle, those who do not use power
or violence to get their way.
The world needs more of them.

I know people who need many supports for living
but who are fine citizens as much for what they don't do
as for what they do.
They don't harbor grudges against their neighbors;
throw trash along the road;
write ugly letters to the newspaper;
drive drunk or shoplift.

Such folks are often looked down on by those
who know how to use force to get what they want.
Communities need the gentle of heart
to temper and redeem the harsher qualities
that people with more abilities bring to our world.

Happy is the milkweed
unnoticed until pods explode
and angels wing forth
seeding the earth.

CHRIS has a gardener's heart. He sees the earth as a garden in danger. Environmental concerns sprinkle his talk: soil and air pollution, acid rain, animal extinction.

Asked how he keeps his houseplants flourishing, he answers simply, "I water them."

He is seen touching the leaves, testing the soil for dryness when he is around plants.

Because he also loves flowers, I asked him to bring a couple mums from the flowerbed at his home for the table at Faith and Light meeting.

He hesitated.
I wondered.
He explained.

"Flowers die when you pick them."

Oh. Of course. I hadn't thought how it would hurt him to pick a flower knowing he was cutting it off from its source of life.

Still, he wanted to bring a flower to the meeting so he said he would.

The red mum he brought was dried up, nearly dead, the one least painfully sacrificed.

Reverently I placed it on the altar with the Christ candle, icon of another gentle heart.

PAULA's home was at Pennhurst before she came to Indian Creek. Pennhurst is marked as one of the largest and most notorious of state institutions where people were warehoused, forgotten for lifetimes. Paula lost her twin sister in infancy, then her father. Her mother, ill, was unable to care for Paula whose severe cerebral palsy required much attention. In the midst of loneliness and indignities, Paula gained faith and patience.

I watched that patience, and persistence as well, as she worked at her workshop job of putting sponges into little net bags for a distributor. Bent over in her wheelchair, her left hand severely limited, she kept on slowly, slowly easing the sponge into the bag until it was finished. Immediately she reached for another.

Though she has learned to use her power-driven chair and can now move from one place to another by herself, her disabilities require waiting for help with most other functions of living.

We were roommates at Faith and Light retreat. She was kind about my fumbling attempts to assist her. In spite of my awkwardness, she remained good-humored and patient. About 2:00 a.m. I awakened to hear her voice softly calling me.

"Yes, Paula, what is it?"

"My covers. I need them pulled up."

As I tucked the blankets in around her shoulders, she explained, "I kept talking to my covers but they just wouldn't answer me."

O*RLANDO,* at the age of 25, was admitted to a large state hospital. The hospital was his home for the next 42 years. He carried with him the huge stoic silence of his past as he came to his new home at Indian Creek.

Knowing of his religious roots in a small Mennonite congregation, I took him there to Sunday morning worship.

He said nothing.

He showed no expression of recognition as we entered and sat on the back bench.

But when the hymn-singing started, the tears started too. They rolled eloquently down his lined and bewhiskered face.

Later "Landy" took to singing:
"The Hobo Song"
"What a Friend We Have In Jesus"
"Let Me Call You Sweetheart"

And he took to smiling.

I watched one of the prettiest of young women staff assistants give him a hug and kiss when she came to pick him up at the Senior Center.

A slow delighted smile transfigured every line of his face.

Inheriting the earth must feel like that.

MARY ANN. To look at her, one would think *meek.* Head bent, eyes downcast. Silent. Mary Ann does not appear to fill the role of a messenger. Mary Ann's messages, however, arrive from the nearly speechless woman in times of need, reminiscent of angelic tidings.

The workshop where Mary Ann works is coordinated by Betty who says worker Mary Ann is orderly to a fault, and diligent. Her communications take the form of drawings left on Betty's desk. Once it was the word "holiday" written over and over. Was Mary Ann needing time off? Betty wondered.

When Mary Ann's sister was hospitalized, the message was Rhonda, Rhonda, Rhonda, Rhonda. And then: "Daddy." And then the single word, "hospital."

Mary Ann's daddy had died in a hospital. Mary Ann was immediately taken to see that her sister was all right, and the relieved embraces and gush of tears were healing for everyone.

Betty had been going through a time of stress with finishing school and questioning whether to apply for a director position, whether to leave altogether for a new job, wanting to stay comfortable and yet wanting to move ahead. She felt insecure and troubled about her future but she kept it undercover, hardly admitting it even to herself.

And then a stunning message arrived on her desk. Written on a scrap of brown paper in pencil was one statement written in five careful lines:

Fear and Panic are your worst enemies
Fear and Panic are your worst enemies
Fear and Panic are your worst enemies
Fear and Panic are your worst enemies
Fear and Panic are your worst enemies

The mystery goes unsolved of where Mary Ann found the words. The result of her message was that Betty regained courage and applied for the position she wanted. She continues as a trusted friend to Mary Ann. Mary Ann has become more free in communication, more free to touch and be touched, more free to ask when she needs something. The prophetic message to her friend hangs framed above Betty's desk.

Blessed is the quiet strength of a Mary Ann.
Such power is changing the world.

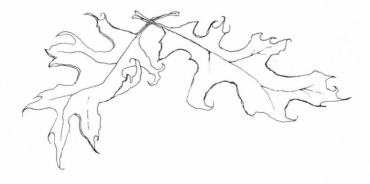

4

Blessed are those who hunger and thirst for righteousness, for they will be filled.

Righteousness. Justice. Goodness.
A world where the good life in its truest meaning
comes to everyone.
In moments when my own life seems almost
too good, too rich to deserve,
I inevitably think of someone in the throes of anguish.
But to let all of the pain and terror of the world's
bad news into one's heart at once
would be enough to freeze it forever.

Blessed are those who long for good things for the
world's people, for all creation, and who include
themselves in the longing.

As one would yearn for food and water after days of
deprivation, so may we yearn for the coming into
fullness of God's just and peaceable reign.
Someday such hunger will be satisfied.

Happy are those
who yearn for good things
they shall be silky
as buttercups.

JOYCE carried a gigantic Bible under her arm everywhere she went (it was blue to match her eyes).

She was baptized and rebaptized because she loved baptisms, giving her testimony, and being welcomed into a new church. Four churches welcomed her in her adult life, and she found a place to be an active participant in them all.

For years, every time she'd see me she'd say, "Barbara! I want to be a Preacher Woman. I know I can do it."

I knew as well that she could do it. Such eagerness to pray, sing, and yes, preach, burst from her hunger to express her love for God.

The fervor of her prayers carried me giddily to the throne of grace.

In her last congregation before she died she was designated Offering Plate Holder for the Sunday morning offertory prayer. She stood ceremoniously at the altar holding the plates. Her eyes closed. A hungry and holy expression transfixed her face.

Happy are you, Joyce, filled now to bursting with God's heavenly many-course banquet.

Barbara has Prader-Willi Syndrome, a chromosomal birth disorder. The most difficult symptom is constant hunger. To stay alive, Barbara must live on a 1000-calorie-a-day diet. Besides this trouble, she has had hospitalizations for serious injuries in a motor accident, diabetes, infections, and heart failure. She lives with a constant frustration that most of us can't even imagine.

Are you ever mad at God for all these troubles?
"Not at God; mad at the Devil. God never hurts us," said Barbara confidently.

She spoke the poetry of praise:

"God has given me
a place to live, a job,
the earth to live on,
trees, breezes, clouds, water, Spirit,
lots of things to do,
faith in myself too."

And what about that constant yearning for food?
"Heaven will be all the food I want."
Like?
"Chicken, mashed potatoes, pie…and spinach," she added, as though remembering righteousness.

LINDA walks the two blocks to church from her group home. She's an hour early, but she has things to do.

In the silence and solitude of the building, she gets things set up for Sunday School coffee time.

She begins putting inserts into the bulletins.

She gets ready to welcome and greet all who arrive after her for the morning worship.

For fifteen years Linda has come to church every Sunday except for when summer camp, injury, or illness kept her away.

Her enthusiastic affection can lift people off their feet as it did when she lifted her tall male and surprised pastor off the floor with an enormous hug.

Though her seizures can be sudden and hard, she risks carrying the microphone around during congregational sharing time and helping to collect offerings.

Her church family takes the risk too of the possible disruption of worship during a seizure.

But Linda has found a spiritual home with real brothers and sisters who know her and care for her.

For Linda, God is known through people, "God with skin on." Her hunger for relationships is also her hunger for the love of God.

In her Sunday School class she listed the people who are her best friends: Dave, Becky, Bob, Anne, Greg, Virgil, Linda, Mark, Ken, all members of the family of God at Perkasie Mennonite Church.

S*TERLING* was sure he was Jewish.

"My mother was Jewish. I'm Jewish," he insisted.
His sister said no one in the family was Jewish.

That didn't stop Sterling. He went to synagogue
with his Jewish friends.

He wore his kippah proudly. Said the prayers.
Conversed with the rabbi.

Sterling won out.

Though he was unable to go through the conversion
process and become officially a Jew, Sterling grasped
where the real authority lay.

"I am Jewish in my heart," he said.

⌘⌘⌘

B*OB* has been a Mormon for thirty years, a Mormon
who combines righteousness with merriment. Bob
chuckles a great deal.

But attaining righteousness is a felt need and he obeys
the rules: no tea, coffee, alcohol. He prays every morning on the
telephone with a brother or sister Mormon to help
keep the faith.

(He intends to pray ten times a day but doesn't
make it.)

He's exempt from tithing though because his
workshop job barely keeps him in pocket change.

Because of his faithfulness he is an elder, a visitor
of others to see if they have needs that should be passed
on to the bishop.

He's the prayer chairman of his elder quorum,
choosing who will lead the closing prayer.

But loneliness is a hunger.

Mormon families have Family Home Evenings
to keep them strong. Bob lives with a housemate and has a
woman friend, but it's not the same.

So, (he grins over this) he watches wrestling instead.

"It's hard to be righteous when you're single," he
says. Being righteous means to honor your membership
and keep to the true and narrow way.

"I almost died three times."

Bob looks at me slyly.

"But God kept me alive to teach you the Word."

He bursts into uproarious laughter.

⌘⌘⌘

I'm thankful that I go to church on Sunday,
I'm thankful that I can believe in God,
and I wish God would help my brother and sister-in-law
to go to church,
and when people get sick or have cancer that God
would help them out to get better and get strong,
and I believe in having friends
and I like to walk around, I do.
If I get real sick I know that God
will help me.   Amen

—Carol

5

Blessed are the merciful,
for they will receive mercy.

"The quality of mercy is not strained," says Shakespeare.
"it droppeth as the gentle rain from heaven…"
Such mercy finds its way out through memory.
Memory of the experience of being forgiven,
of being offered not what I deserve, but what will heal
me. Like a slow spring rain warming the frozen earth,
mercy brings greening to hearts that have gone cold.
Asking for mercy may not bring it about;
mercy, like forgiveness, wants to be offered freely.
There is no bargaining. Mercy is pure gift.
And as Shakespeare goes on to say,
"it blesseth him that gives and him that takes."

Happy are the merciful
covering bare patches like clover
growing strong where there's hurt
green as the hands of rain.

*R*ON found a kitten in a paper bag beside the road.

An abandoned kitten ought surely to ensure mercy. Except that someone *left* the kitten in a paper bag beside the road, a person, no doubt, of at least average intellectual capacities. The workshop crew picking up litter found it. Ron opened the bag. The tiny scared creature could not have looked up into a more compassionate face.

Ron comes with my husband and me to church. It all takes time. The pleasantries of good morning, handshakes, inquiries of our health, helping us with doors, coats and bulletins all take up time that is best known as Sabbath time. Time for reverence and reflection. Time for caring.

A large circle is gathered for the Sunday School discussion in the fellowship hall. Virginia is late, and with all chairs filled, sits on the steps that lead to the worship room. On the other side of the circle, Ron's heart moves quickly from concern to action.

Because of disabled legs, he moves in small stiff steps, *tink, tink,* as one Ron-admirer describes. Time waits while the teacher fills in and all eyes follow Ron. Around the circle he goes to the big chair rack, removing a chair as unclatteringly as possible, carrying it to Ginnie and offering it.

An appreciative sigh follows him slowly back around the circle to his own chair.

Would that our lesson stay with us that morning: Taking Time for Mercy.

ED comes with a tentative knock on the door of the
office. He's come again with his requests for prayer.
What world catastrophe this time, or American misfortune,
or friend in trouble?

Big Ed folds his big hands, bows his head and
shuts his eyes. Right there in the doorway with other
people coming and going, Ed wants to pray for the
sufferers of the world.
Oklahoma City receives his supplications.
TWA Flight 800.
Bosnians.
Princess Di.
The baby beaten by her father.
All victims of earthquake, flood and famine.

The mercy of Ed's heart promises mercy for Ed.
When he badly needs a cigarette, let one be given.
When he walks to WaWa for coffee, let him be
kindly served.

Let the mercy he gives rise like a cloud
and rain on his earnest, petitioning head.

⌘⌘⌘

Our Father who art in heaven
Hallowed be thy name
Thy will be done
In Jesus' name, Amen.
Bless my dad, his surgery went good and he's home again
and he's coming to visit on Tuesday night.
Bless everybody in the hospital, God,
and at the old folks' home.   Amen

                              —Ed

MILDRED was one of a dozen who traveled to Winnipeg, Canada, one summer for a four-day international retreat on disability. Overseeing our Indian Creek gang was much more than I could handle, but I didn't know it at the time. Only after I was in over my head did I know.

In the thick of the unmanageable chaos of airports and luggage, transportation to the college, money exchange, dormitory mazes and cafeteria lines, Mildred was a rock of consolation. Seventy and white-haired, she was also calm, funny, and dependable. She helped keep me sane throughout the entire melee.

On the last evening she topped it all with a scene from the Last Supper.

The exhausting day over, I dropped on the bed in the room we were sharing.

Mildred came over and picked up my sweaty and aching feet.

She began to massage.

Like Peter, I protested.

Like Jesus, she laughed and kept on.

Mildred the merciful. Blessed are your strong and gentle hands, your healing laughter.

6

Blessed are the pure in heart,
for they will see God.

Purity of heart is to will one thing, says Kierkegaard.
Singleheartedness in *seeking* God leads to *seeing* God.
Do we know that when we are pursuing some
unworthy goal it is more likely God that we seek?

An honest heart will eventually lead to the Creator of
the heart. Honesty is often a gift of those with mental
disabilities. The honesty may be received as rude or
refreshing. Once I was told by a hospitalized core
member I'd come to see, "Shut up and go away!" I was
refreshed. Polite endurance is not helpful in
knowing how to provide chaplaincy services. But that
same honesty doesn't shy away from strong expressions
of love. Deep affection rises purely from the pure in heart.
The unmasked face shall surely behold the friendly
face of God.

Happy is the daisy
a golden eye
fringed in white lashes
watching heaven, seeing God.

D*ICK* comes to mind when it's time to plan a funeral. His "Amazing Grace" solos bring on the healing tears. One middle-aged staff person has already contracted with Dick to sing "Amazing Grace" at his memorial service. It would not be a bad idea to have Dick touring the country singing "Amazing Grace" at all funerals.

Purity of heart, genuine and simple faith pour out. He doesn't put on airs. He stands and belts it out, and if one phrase gets exchanged for another, no problem. It's probably better that way anyway.

Dick's enthusiastic faith leads him to appreciate all faiths. Though he's active in an independent Bible congregation, he loves going to a Mennonite church, a Jewish synagogue, a Catholic mass. The joyful worship of one God is his creed.

Dick and I went together to an all-day conference on disabilities which ended in the evening with a prayer and healing service. We were to stand and sing as people went forward for prayer. I was getting tired as the meeting went on and on.

I wanted to sit down. Stop singing. Go home. But Dick's sixty years of energy and pleasure never dimmed. And so, to keep up with him, I held on to the very last note.

At the Amen, Dick turned to me with more joyful possibilities. "Hey, Barbara, let's stop on the way home for coffee!"

D_{ELLA}'s pure heart gleamed with an honest and accepting self-identity.

"I am a retarded girl," she told a camp counselor.

"Oh well, Della, everyone has some kind of handicap," the counselor countered.

"Really?" asked the direct Della. "What is yours?"

Her "I am" pronouncements were often meant to be entryways into some desired adventure.

"I am a Youth," meant "I can go to church youth camp."

"I am a Woman," meant "I can go to Women's Retreat."

She assessed others with the same free acceptance. "You are an Old Lady; you have wrinkles," she kept her grandmother informed, stroking the appraised condition.

Della had Cyto Magallic Inclusion Body Disorder. "CID" kept her delayed in self-help skills, but brightly progressing in reading and retention skills.

She carried with her three books at a time, her "companions," and stupified her parents and friends with trivia from the Civil War, the Bible, church history, and every American president.

New words fascinated her. "Discretion," her mother said. "Use discretion at the salad bar."

When Della caught on, she ran shrieking through the restaurant to the amazement of other patrons.

"Mommy, Mommy, I used discretion!"

At five, she was found standing on a Bible in the living room dramatizing a Sunday School chorus, "I stand alone on the Word of God."

Public education gave up and sent her to private school after a series of mishaps; the final one was getting her arm caught in a downspout. Cooking oil released the arm in the musical dramatization of the little creature who climbs up the water spout.

Della fell into a coma at the age of twenty-five and died three months later of herpes encephalitis.

Seeing God had come easily for her… in people, nature, her dog, Shadow, in the serendipity of each day.

Della was a daisy.
Fresh, open, her heart exuberantly
in love with life.

M_{ARK}'s interest in heaven became acute when his only brother died at a youthful age. Questions about heaven got intense. Especially intense was his concern whether his favorite things would be there.

One day it was about Nintendo. Our Nintendo dialogue resolved within myself a question that had long troubled me.

"Barbara, will there be Nintendo in heaven?"

I don't know, Mark, but whatever you need to be happy God will give you.

"But will there be Nintendo there?"

Mark, when you were a baby you needed a bottle. Do you want a bottle now?

"No."

So maybe when we get to heaven we won't want what we do now.

"But will there be Nintendo in heaven?"

If you need Nintendo in heaven to be happy, Yes, Mark, there will be Nintendo in heaven.

I have never rested assured that I would be with those I love in heaven. Mark gave back to me my own words.

Barbara, if you must have the presence of your loved ones in heaven in order to be happy, God will provide it.

Thanks, Mark, that's what I needed.

Four Women

To protect their identities, I will call them rivers: Colorado, Mississippi, Ohio, and Arkansas. They run deep and shallow, muddy and clear, smooth and wild. They are what they are. They roll along engaging shores.

Colorado was born "normal." Her father frequented bars and beat her. He beat her on the head until she was brain damaged and diagnosed with epilepsy. The seizures had her parents disliking her even more. Finally the county took her off their hands.

Mississippi was born with a quirk in her genes. "Downs," the physical symptoms announced at birth. Her parents were genteel people, committed to nice living. Mississippi was kept nicely, taught and trained to a gracious life. As a teen, she rebelled until she was mercifully taken in by plain folks who felt called to serve people like her.

Ohio was a mystery. What happened no one knows, but she was a curly-haired cutie pie and easy to care for until she reached adolescence and was beset by storm. Again the county came to fix and fixed her with a multitude of services until she broke away from them all and catapulted herself into freedom. Freedom to ruin her life if and as she pleased.

Arkansas was a baby with a double whammy; diabetes along with what had gotten crimped in her brain. She was born angry. Her anger fattened. Her voice got harsh. Early, she was taken from her mother for "professional attention." Between insulin shots and community glares, Arkansas fumed until the day she met a sweet little man who wasn't afraid of her, who agreed to marry her and did. Then she calmed, sometimes, just a bit.

These women, these rivers run through my life. They inspire me, frustrate, trick, and teach me. They are called mentally retarded or intellectually disabled or developmentally challenged. But they are women pushing against enormous barriers who do not give up. They just keep rolling along.

Colorado regularly falls over like a struck tree. A crowd gathers. A panicky bystander calls an ambulance. But then she is on her feet, laughing, shrugging off the humiliation, and on her way.

Mississippi says, "Oh well, that's life," when one of her best laid dream projects gets squashed. And then she goes on to the next with the same well-mannered, determined will.

Ohio courts trouble. All who know her throw up their hands. Something must be done. But what? In the meantime she survives. She dances in the park. She carries her world in a big greasy handbag and her self in her small pert street-wise body.

Arkansas's anger keeps her voiced ragged. She sees people turn away. She doesn't give a damn, expressing herself as she will. Her loyalty to her man is power, a sermon for the marriages of her congregation of case managers, medical advisors, and counselors.

Sometimes I stand on the banks to watch these rivers. Sometimes I wade in and get refreshed or knocked down and nearly drowned. Sometimes I try to channel just a bit of the flow in a new direction with hardly any effect.

Mostly I consider what these rivers are and feel amazed. Strong, stubborn, wise, unique. Pure in heart. Women to respect, admire and love.

7

Blessed are the peacemakers,
for they will be called children of God.

How much of the strife in this world is the result
of competition? Getting my share.
Claiming my prize. Beating out my opponents.
In a Special Olympics race, with the finishing line
coming up, one runner stumbled, began to cry.
The runners near him stopped. Helped him up.
Encouraged him to keep going.
Only then did they continue the race together.
Peacemakers are not discriminators.
Weeds and royals get the same respect.
The temptation is subtle to give our attention to those
of notable status, while ignoring small powerless ones.
Peacemaking takes courage.
In our culture where winning and success
are more desirable than friendship,
choosing to give our best to relationships
may seem absurd and self-defeating.
But I have learned from my disabled friends the value
of simple affection.
Peacemakers bless the world with the healing power
of their love.

Happy are the peacemakers
like the lace of Queen Anne
bringing weed and royalty together
as children of God.

R*ICHARD*'s smile is wide and dimpled. He thinks about things. Things like what to do about violence in the world. "Here's what we should do, Barbara," he says. "First we turn all the gun shops into hobby shops."

He gazes at me to see if I'm following him.

Great idea, Richard.

"Then we dig a very big hole and bury all the guns."

A wonderful idea, Richard. Big enough to bury the bombs, missiles, fighter planes, aircraft carriers, and the Pentagon too?

⌘⌘⌘

M*ARY KATHRYN* is helping lay out on the table the name tags for Faith and Light meeting. She is a quiet little Mennonite woman, her white prayer covering on her head, dignified but friendly. Noise erupts in the circle of people already seated. Henry has arrived upset. He yells and shakes a fist. Those nearby cannot soothe him.

Mary Kathryn says, "Maybe if I take him his name tag he'll feel better." I wonder if this will be good for Mary Kathryn. But I agree that it's worth a try.

She carries the name tag into the fray and holds it out. He stops yelling and reaches out his arms and clasps them tightly around her neck. I watch, praying that she can stay with him and not get scared. She stays. Finally he lets go and settles back in peace.

Mary Kathryn returns to the table with a satisfied smile. Courageous peacemaker, the admired of God.

LEONARD is on his big three-wheeler inching along Route 113. To watch him in all weather, waving to his friends in trucks, school buses, and cars is to watch a peacemaker in action.

A huge American flag flies above his seat. He wears a helmet, sunglasses and a large toothless smile.

The community recognizes Leonard. A newspaper story of his minor accident brought calls asking "Is Leonard okay?"

Leonard never learned to talk. In state hospitals for most of his life, he learned to communicate through gestures. But he learned enough to manage a trash recycling business and make friends. His bike cart is soon filled with aluminum cans from businesses, churches, and roadsides along his extensive route.

He can order breakfast in the local diner by mimicking a chicken and raising fingers for how many eggs.

Leonard is a welcomed presenter in a series called, "Straight from the Heart." He is accompanied to schools, clubs, and congregations to tell his life story. Though grizzled gray, Leonard is especially favored by elementary school children who give him rousing ovations.

His friendly face and sturdy physical frame make him a perfect Santa Claus at Christmas. "Ho, Ho, Ho," he can say clearly and clearly, Leonard brings a fresh dimension to peacemaking as he travels harmoniously about his community.

LAVERNE, PAUL, WILLIAM. Three gray-haired

brothers come into the Faith and Light meeting and sit
down in a row like a trinity of saints. Their presence
evokes peace. Gentle, dignified, and devout, they
nevertheless join in the lively singing with rhythm
instruments (to their own beat).

Laverne takes the lead with Paul and William in tow.
They all live in a retirement community and leave the
meeting early because they are concerned they could
be locked out of their building at night.

They talked with me about peace and peacemaking.
They took turns answering my questions.

What do you think peacemaking is all about?

"It's about peace with God and peace with other
people."

What do you need in order to be a peacemaker?

"You need love. You need patience."

*You all seem like very peaceful people. Does
anything upset or annoy you?*

(One brother gets annoyed in the dining room when a
fellow diner takes too much sugar. Another has a room-
mate who turns off the light too soon.)

What do you do if an argument is going on?

"I stop talking whenever there's an argument."

When you were little boys in your family, did you
fight with each other?

"I think we did, as children do." Laverne smiles a bit
ruefully.

"But now we ought to put away childish things!" Paul
declared suddenly and emphatically, quoting the
Apostle with the same name who wrote those words to
the Church of the Corinthians.

Immersed in a "peace" church since babyhood,
these brothers know the Bible, love their Lord, and
bless a world desperately in need of their way of peace.

⌘⌘⌘

Oh my God,
Bless this spring,
Bless Barbara as she tapes this,
Bless David and Steve that he doesn't shake so much,
that he can go places,
Bless the times we have together at Indian Creek
having a fun time,
Bless the prayer group I'm in at my church,
and bless all the people at the group home,
We're doing a good job,
really good.

In Jesus' name, Amen.

—Richard

8

Blessed are those who are persecuted
for righteousness sake,
for theirs is the kingdom of heaven.

Blessed are those who are ill-treated through no sins
of their own. The abused abound in the world of
mental retardation. From neighborhoods that fight to
keep out a group home, to the subtle turning away of
the person seated next in a waiting room, these artless
ones are seldom treated as who Jesus says they are…
royal heirs. The persecutions hardest to accept are
those that come from the people of God.

Rejections are painful. With limited choices at hand,
persons with disabilities find self-esteem floundering.
No wonder there is a great sadness mixed in with
their joy. The prophet Micah promises that someday
all people shall sit under their own vines and fig trees,
and no one shall make them afraid. Let it be soon.

Happy are the creatures
who must hide to survive
the kingdom of heaven
shall be their home.

TRISH has a voice like a bell. Young and sweet-faced, she would quickly find a church home, or so I imagined. But finding a congregation willing to welcome a disabled person into their worship and community is a challenge. The slogans, the theology, the mission statements too often fall short of opening the doors to those who need support in worship.

Trish is blind. She needed to be guided, and she made rhythmic movements and occasional soft sounds as she sat on the pew during our hopeful visit to a thriving evangelical church.

The singing was lively. Trish's silvery voice rang out on the chorus:

Shine, Jesus, shine,
Lift our hearts to the Father's glory.
Glow, Spirit, glow,
Set our hearts on fire.

I was proud to be with her, eager to have her connected and loved in this congregation.

But the weeks and months dragged on after our Sunday morning visit with no response to my request for a helper. Finally the pastor called to explain that no one was available to bring Trish to church. Sorry.

Glow, Sprit, glow,
Set our hearts on fire...

B_{RAD} loves music; Luciano Pavarotti is his favorite singer. Brad's own repertoire ranges from "O Holy Night" to "Here Comes The Bride."

Born and raised in the Jewish faith, Brad also knows many of the Hebrew songs and chants of his religious heritage. A sober young man, he rarely smiles, but his pleasure in synagogue worship was easy to see… less easy to listen to because Brad's musical key is monotone. Loud monotone.

Even so, it was a joy to take him to Friday evening Shabbat services. We tried to sit where other worshippers wouldn't be bothered. I tried to persuade him to sing more softly and stop when the cantor stopped. But Brad needed to sing a few notes behind the congregation, and since the congregation on Friday evenings was rather sparse, Brad's Hebrew singing was quite distinguishable.

The rabbi was supportive. Brad was a true worshipper. He knew what this was about. His heart was in it. He was welcome.

But one evening after the service an irate woman ripped into Brad and his escort. Speaking for the congregation, she insisted he was disruptive and was completely ruining the worship for everyone. He should not be allowed to attend.

Blessed are you, Brad, son of a King and heir to the Kingdom. May you sing someday before God's throne to thunderous applause.

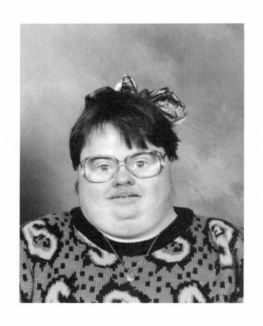

Dear L L son
Mayor

you were nagging about in 1941 I grand gethem
when I was little you heard nothing about
disabled or Retarded or what they call some people
you were talking about nobody what they need
well my Brother Robie Carl off my Business
Because I am on Disability Because they think I
am dumb Because I cannot Change money
but no one is trying to help me and I have
no job Because I don't have no schooling
That I should of had and gone up in trying to
get a job Because no body wants me
and if I remember right Driftian Creek started
1975 and I was first there of weather for two half
years and then they put out on own

from C Clifford Swartley

57

We Shall All Kneel

"Shabbat Shalom,"
The usher murmurs, offering programs
for the Friday evening worship.
My three companions accept, settling
yarmulkes on their impaired skulls,
then lope to the front. I nudge
far left, hoping the congregation
won't notice our muddled participation
in welcoming the Sabbath Bride.

These sons of Abraham are helpless
in helping me through their holy tradition.
I try out the books, page backward, forward,
Hebrew and English, stand late, sit early, and
face the rear, Josh chanting loudly while heads
turn, Cantor and Rabbi move fast and I play ping-
pong with my thoughts: shush, don't shush, blush,
don't blush, these are their children, they belong,
Remember Sarah's welcoming tent.

Remember the houses of worship where
Catholic, Baptist, Mennonite, greet and forget
guileless souls who are originals in the Beatitudes
and strangers in the house of the Lord.
Shabbat Shalom, Joshua, chant away and
eat well at the refreshment tables!
We all shall one day bow before one God.
We shall all kneel like children together.

9

You are the salt of the earth.

In our high-tech society, we have forgotten the value
of salt. "Low-salt" is now what we look for.
In biblical times salt preserved what would otherwise
be useless or toxic. Salt also seasons, makes palatable.
On icy sidewalks salt brings safety.

Good people who populate the earth preserve it.
Pray-ers of all faiths, entreating God for peace, help
keep away nuclear Armageddon.

The communities of the world are safer, more palatable
because people with integrity and good will inhabit
them. Among Hebrews, it was a religious custom to
put some salt on newborns to ensure good health.
Persons like Carol, Allen and B.J. offer health to us
all as they live in our communities as the salt of the earth.

CAROL says she doesn't use salt, but she was willing to
think about what being the "salt of the earth" means.
*Salt makes food taste better, Carol. If people were salt,
would the world be better off?*
"If the world was better it would make God feel good."
*What are some things that people could do to make
the world better and God feel good?*
"Love one another; forgive people; believe in him."
How long have you believed in God, Carol?
"Since 1975. A long time. God helps me every day."

ALLEN is a man of times and seasons. He would agree perfectly with the wisdom of the Ecclesiastics writer that for everything there is a season and a time for every purpose under heaven.

There is a time to get ready for bed, and it is wise to be home in time for that time. There is a season for diligent work, beginning at 6:30 a.m., making boxes and packing sausage for Hatfield Packing, followed by the season for daily diversions of gospel music, evening walks with his dad around the retirement home where he lives, and Jeopardy.

Order and rhythm prevail. Under his bed is a box. The box contains years and years of weekly church bulletins copied by hand. This task he says he enjoys. It sharpens his reading and writing skills and keeps him informed of everything that is going on in his congregation.

He was baptized there at age fourteen. The others in the class, more than a dozen teenagers, received instruction, but he got in on his uncatechized faith alone.

"I baptize you in the name of the Father, the Son, and the Holy Ghost," Allen remembers the words. "I said 'yes' to all the questions the pastor asked me. My tie got wet, but I felt good."

Allen's impeccable grooming matches his manners. His parents have trained him well, bolstered by their belief that by looking good and being good he will more likely be acceptable to the community.

Allen has lots of friends; friends of his parents, friends in the retirement home, at church, at work. Does he have a friend his own age to hang out with? Well... there's a guy who likes him a lot, who at Faith and Light meeting rushes to give him a big hug, but Allen's not sure about that. Miss Manners says "Be polite," but public hugging doesn't fit into his order of things.

Allen's sensitivity to the feelings of people came my way during a meeting to discern a new leader for Faith and Light. Many good things were being said about the new leader. The photos were being taken of her. My ten years were history. Feelings were mixed. Then Allen sauntered over next to me, draped an arm casually across my chair, and looked at me closely. "And how are *you* feeling, Barbara?" he asked.

A tranquil life graces Allen with peace and contentment.

Any worries?... No.

Anything you want?... Not really.

Oh, he does remember when his dad had a motorcycle. Riding one of those again would be fun.

There are enough blips in the routine to keep life lively enough: trips to out-of-state sisters, a flight to the west coast and the chance to take the wheel of a motorboat on the Columbia River, reading the Scripture lesson to a big national church conference audience.

Allen's life moves along, seasoned and seasoning. Preserved and preserving. A good man with a good life, just being the salt of the earth.

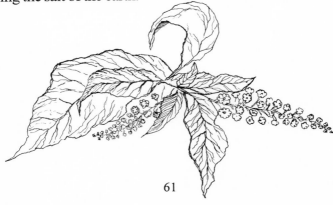

B.J. is in her little rowhouse apartment at noon when I come to visit. Forty-five year-old Billie Joan is as short as her nickname. I watch her move slowly, laboriously, around her kitchen fixing her lunch. I marvel at the way she manages her life. Even though she breathes hard with her exertions, she finally sits down with a big plate of salad and gets to eating. I have to keep responding to her many apologies for eating in front of me... I have eaten, B.J., thank you.

Princess Rose leaps to the table and is welcomed. Gentle is this Queen Mother. A tail curls gracefully around B.J.'s neck. With small, tender hands she removes the cat to the floor. She meant to name the Princess after her favorite Sleeping Beauty character, Princess Aurora, but *Aurora* is just too hard to say.

"The Lord knew I was lonely and gave me the nicest gift of a little animal."

Princess Rose checks all visitors out to see if they are all right. Imagination is a B.J. gift. She writes poems in her journals about friends and candlelight, nightfall by the moon, seeing someone in the corner of a garden, loving your body, and coming to the end of a rainbow valley (on the death of a friend).

Built as she is, she is still able to dance with lightness and grace. "Sacred" dance, she insists, as she twirls a sheer scarf or two. Her hands folded, face turned to heaven, she becomes a priestess entreating God for us all.

Her spontaneous prayers take wings. Calling to say she couldn't come to Faith and Light meeting, she asked to pray with me for the meeting over the telephone. "Close your eyes and fasten your seatbelt," she instructed before she began.

Her baptism is a sweet memory:
"As I was raised up from the stairway,
I saw the Lord raising me up;
Angel wings almost carried me."

Thus she became a "good Christian" and listens to her heart and God at the same time. (I wondered about her walking around town alone at night, but she is confident. "I am not alone; the Lord is with me.") Her baptism hymn was "Amazing Grace," though she asked to change the word *wretch* to *person*. A wretch would be the kind of person who would blind you with a blindfold, she explained.

Deep feelings are a B.J. natural. One poem of hers says, "I am a person with real feelings,
I'd like to tell you some of my feelings."

Tears and laughter run close to the surface. The pain is about relationships, the longing for love—true, romantic love. Boyfriends come and go, but none is a possibility for committed partnership. There is a deep sadness that such longings for a more traditional life of marriage and family, freedom and mobility, are limited by her Downs Syndrome.

The loss of her father when she was 28 and a special woman caregiver, Isabel, are ongoing griefs that recur in conversation, close in memory.

And yet she finds energy and skill to overcome and

make a good life.

She hugs with a breathtaking strength.

She talks to people everywhere she goes, unashamed, unafraid to be herself.

She gives gifts: the shirt off her back literally at a retreat when a child grasped her brightly decorated tee shirt. She offered her own heart to a friend who was threatened with heart failure.

She latch hooks and visits her friends around town and stops in at the pizza shop for lunch. Her part-time job with a cleaning crew is less than rewarding, but she finds consolations along the way in all social opportunities.

Here is a person who lives with love, joy, and courage. A person whose generosity and integrity and self-confidence make the world a better place.

It's time for me to leave... B.J. has fallen asleep in mid-sentence.

And that's another gift: a relaxed pace.

I'll take some B.J. seasoning with me as I go.

10

You are the light of the world.

FAITH AND LIGHT CANDLE

I saw a candle lit in a room,
with all our friends and praying,
one little candle of love is standing,
one little candle of love and happy things.
                                        —*B.J. Diehl*

It was in 1968 that a French Catholic couple with two
disabled sons wished to go to Lourdes on a pilgrimage
to find help for the suffering of their family. They asked
to go with a church group but were told they could not
because of the special needs of their sons.

They decided then to go by themselves. It was a
painful experience. They were not allowed in the hotel
dining room, they were stared at in the places of
worship, and they went home feeling worse than before
they arrived.

Then their paths crossed that of Jean Vanier.
Vanier, a few years earlier, had invited two mentally
handicapped men from an institution to make a home
with him. Vanier understood their pain and
disappointment and decided to organize a pilgrimage
especially for disabled children, their parents and friends.

This event took three years to plan. More and more people heard of it and more and more wanted to go along. Finally they numbered 12,000 people. The group was divided into small groups to pray and prepare. At last, in 1971, they were ready to go.

For three days the town of Lourdes was transformed by a miracle of love and celebration as people with many different disabilities were welcomed. Families and friends shared in the joy of being together to worship, pray, and rejoice. On the last day of the pilgrimage, the question was heard, "What are we going to do now?"

Jean Vanier gathered the community leaders together and said, "What we have been given is so precious that it must not be lost. Let us let love show us what to do next."

So the little community groups that had gotten together to prepare for the pilgrimage continued to meet and pray and share their faith and love. These groups multiplied into an international organization called "Faith and Light" that today numbers over 1,200 communities in 70 countries.

What is the attraction? What does Faith and Light have to offer?

Faith and Light believes that each person, however profoundly he or she may be disabled, is called to be a source of grace and peace for the whole community, for the Church, and for all humanity. The Charter goes on to say, "In a society based on usefulness and power, people with mental handicaps may not be efficient, but they are nonetheless prophetic in the area of the heart and of tenderness, and in what is essential in the human person."

So the heart of Faith and Light is "beatitude" people. The poor in spirit, the mourners, the meek, those who hunger for justice, the merciful, the pure in heart, the peacemakers and the persecuted... the ones who are open to God's values, and who show the way to the kingdom of heaven.

Welcome is the first gift at a Faith and Light group meeting. Each person must be received with a name tag, a handshake or hug, a smile, and a lively song. We sit in a circle with the Faith and Light candle glowing to make music, pray, participate in story and mime. Sharing the joys and sorrows of our lives leads to honest prayers. We celebrate with games, snacks, and special events like picnics and birthday parties. Spring and fall retreats take us to other settings for strengthening our relationships and our purpose.

A Faith and Light meeting at Indian Creek was described like this:

"L. lights the Jesus candle tonight. He surprises me by pulling out a cigarette lighter instead of taking the match I'm holding. But the candle is lit. Now we sit in a circle of silence. We welcome Jesus to Faith and Light.

"B. always asks for prayer for his mother. If there's been a national disaster or serious accident, prayers rise powerfully. Once when prayer was suggested for a newly engaged couple, C. leaped to her feet and danced in the circle. She is the same person who runs with a comforting hug if someone begins to weep.

"Singing sets everyone in motion. D., who speaks so haltingly that he may bend to the floor with the effort, stand up and lets loose a grand hymn without a hitch. Clapping, red crepe paper streamers, rhythm instruments, laughing, dancing, and shouting are acceptable musical accompaniment.

"The best stories are the impromptu dramas. *Jesus* lounges on the floor beside a bright cloth. His disciples hang around watching a beshawled woman spray perfume on the head of their friend. She is solemn and reverent. They grin and nudge each other. The fragrance of the costly gift fills the room. When the story's over everyone bows to the applause."

Faith and Light is the world-wide community of differing cultures, languages and races, even religions, all held together by the deep love of God that comes from the hearts of persons with developmental disability. Faith and Light brings together family and friends to support and care for each other in a unique setting. Faith and Light is the one small meeting of a handful of persons celebrating their commitment to one another and God around "one little candle of love and happy things."

I know your kingdom is for us,
the Bible tells me so,
and little ones unto him,
into the gate of your kingdom
and your pasture.
I saw a light,
in it a child was walking
to see God.
She was happy.

Thank you, God. Amen

—*B.J. Diehl*

It is very well to say that people with mental retardation love God and have spiritual gifts to offer the community. It is quite a different thing to welcome them into our congregations as full members.

The good life for persons with developmental disabilities includes valued membership in a religious community, says Wolf Wolfensberger, recognized leader in the field of mental retardation. Even the experts at American Association on Mental Retardation now call for religous supports.

In one professional journal, two Ph.Ds wrote that there is a need to "systematically incorporate" the development of religious and spiritual life into the experience of persons with mental retardation.

Disabled persons need to participate in a full range of human experiences. Congregations are blessed with such a range: birth and death, fellowship and conflict, work and worship, the suffering and celebration of what it means to be human beings committed to God and one another.

Persons who live in group homes may not have the opportunity to be with little children. In the congregation they meet a family with a new baby. They may assist in the nursery and make friends with old people. In sharing the joys and sorrows of life in the congregation, they have a richer and fuller life.

The congregation is also the place to share their gifts. Religious communities have typically felt called to serve the needy, but a basic need for all of us is to have our gifts called forth and welcomed.

The gift may be the gift of friendliness. The congregation could say, "Your gift can be used in greeting those who come to worship, in visiting the elderly, in mailing out newsletters." Nothing is so affirming and stimulating as being asked to use gifts in ministry to others.

Faith communities can use the gifts of spontaneous, openhearted people. Do we tend to stuffiness? We can learn to lighten up. Do we suffer from intellectualism, self-sufficiency, perfectionism? The gifts of our brothers and sister who are mentally disabled can help us.

The congregation can also offer continuity of relationships for those who live in group homes. Unfortunately, staffing changes often. Support people come and go; relationships are lost. In a congregation, relationships are more likely to remain stable and long-term.

So, if the congregation is willing to reach out to welcome people with mental retardation into their midst, what is the next step?

Assess the present group. There may well be disabled members of families still hidden from view. There may be those on the fringes, forgotten because of disability. Intentional leadership is needed to find and begin the task of including. Group homes in the area would no doubt be amazed and delighted to have a representative from the local faith community stop in to visit and invite residents to worship services.

Training is available for the congregation in how to care for people who have special needs. Books, educational materials and resource persons are available from many national denominational offices. Ginny Thornburgh of the National Organization on Disability, Religious Division, in Washington, D.C. offers workshops, books, and guidance.

But inclusion will need to begin small, possibly with one person. There is no substitute for learning to know this one individual, making a place for the welcome of this child of God. Adapting comes too. Acceptance and flexibility will be required. The faith community exists to serve God by serving people.

For Christians, we cannot be the Body of Christ unless those who are judged weaker are honored with the honor of the whole. In this meadow of the kingdom of God, we join together in our many differences and likenesses, to fulfill God's creative will for a grace-filled universe.

Addresses of Interest

Ginny Thornburgh
National Organization On Disability
910 Sixteenth Street, NW
Washington, D.C. 10006

Maureen O'Reilly
Faith and Light International Coordinator
1428 Elm St.
Dearborn, Michigan 48124